Life and Dea

Palmwine Sounds

Copyright © 2024 Palmwine Publishing Limited Nigeria
All rights reserved. No part of this publication may be reproduced, distributed, or transmitted in any form or by any means, including photocopying, recording, or other electronic or mechanical methods, without the prior written permission of the publisher, except in the case of brief quotations embodied in critical reviews and certain other non-commercial uses permitted by copyright law.

Author- Palmwine Sounds
Illustrator- Arts Reginald

ISBN (Paperback)- 978-1-917267-30-4

ISBN (E-Book)- 978-1-917267-31-1

Published by Nubian Republic on behalf of Raffia Press Nigeria Limited and imprint of Palmwine Publishing Limited Nigeria

Email: info@palmwinepublishing.com

Address- UK: 86-90, Paul Street, London EC2A 4NE

Address-Nigeria: 1A Jos Road Bukuru, Plateau State, Nigeria.

www.palmwinepublishing.com
www.raffiapress.com
www.nuciferaanalysis.com

Life and Death by Palmwine Sounds

TABLE OF CONTENTS

The Game	1
Cruise	2
Trouble	3
Wicked Ones	3
Men of Culture	4
Odogwu	5
Idan	5
Baddo	6
Dancing	7
Lit am!!!	8
Respect	9
Zion	9
Wicked Kingdom	9
Condition	10
Jah Rastafari	10
Badman Lighter	11
Baba	12
Youths	12
Creators	13
Pain	14
Chaos Show	15
Being a Man	15
Mistakes	16
Ginger	17
Fisher Men	17
Hustlers	18
Wicked Game	18
Rest	19
Marijuana	20
Different Shades	21
God dey Create	22
Jah Guides	23
Jah Jah Blesses	24

Life and Death by Palmwine Sounds

Praise Jah	--------------------	24
Not Ordinary	--------------------	24
Father	--------------------	25
Otedola	--------------------	26
Beauty	--------------------	27
American Military	--------------------	27
Stubborness	--------------------	27
Knackademos	--------------------	28
True Madness	--------------------	29
Drum and bass	--------------------	29
Trust	--------------------	30
Ikebe	--------------------	31
Holy Mount Zion	--------------------	32
Ghana Men	--------------------	32
Cruise Nation	--------------------	32
Wahala	--------------------	33
Funk	--------------------	34
Jah Soldiers	--------------------	34
Heavy Rotation	--------------------	35
No Condition is Permanent	--------------------	36
Smile	--------------------	37
Yansh is my Religion	--------------------	38
Ashawo	--------------------	39
The Most High	--------------------	40
Sunday Rice	--------------------	41
Living The Highlife	--------------------	41
Hushpuppy	--------------------	42

Life and Death by Palmwine Sounds

The Game

In this game of life and death

I do not play only chess

Include checkers on one board

My moves become unpredictable.

Cruise

The rawest form of happiness
With it, man shall never be weary
Downpression 'scorned' away
Sufferation 'scorned' away
Just pray and smile problems away.

Trouble

Look for Trouble's trouble
You would collect double

For every action
A double reaction

Odugwu Fela vibration
Madmen mentalities

Longing for chaos
Present opportunities

Wicked Ones

They shall reign for a little
When justice calls
Hammer shall respond

Tread with the wicked
All shall follow suit
No mercy shall be given.

Wicked begets wickedness
Wuta (fire) Wuta (fire) season
Flog them in nah the Babylon

Men of Culture

Appreciate God's Creations
Were two or three men gather
Women must be discussed

Be it yansh, breast, thighs…
Mannerisms, personality…
Deliberate and appreciate.

Life and Death by Palmwine Sounds

Odogwu

I am Fashionably late
As I Waka for stage
The stage goes bengdedegen
Raining insults at the crowd
Respond by hailing me
The cruise machine spinning.

Idan

Idan is a man of peace
Idan does not fight
Idan comes and goes as he pleases
Idan is everywhere and no where
Idan no like stress
Idan communicates directly with God
Idan life is fuelled of Cruise

Baddo

Baba for the Boys
No need for introduction
His grass nah your grace
He chops. We chop
Men prostrate in his presence
Cruise throws Salute.

Dancing

One leg up
One leg down

Two leg up
Two leg down

One hand up
One hand down

Two hands up
Two hand down

Shake your body
Nah your own

Body dey inside cloth
Dey Gbedu dey enter

Feel the bassline
Dance to the drums

Life and Death by Palmwine Sounds

Lit am!!!

Lend me your fire!!!
Have the herb ready
Ignite the packed roll
All sorrows disappear
Even if for a little while.

Gives me inspiration
Make me feel wavy
Fights Downpression
Ignores Sufferation
The international herb!!!

Respect

Show me respect
I shall reciprocate

Show me disrespect
To me you don't exist

My eye contact with me
All shall see is rudeness

Zion

Zion is a holy place
Zion is a peaceful place

Zion has no sin
Zion has no wicked

Zion is a place of love
Zion is a joyous place

Zion has no downpression
Zion has no sufferation.

Wicked kingdom

Wicked kingdom shall fall
Like the walls of Jericho
False hope shall reside within
Like a losing army in battle
Back facing the enemy
While destruction flies by.

Life and Death by Palmwine Sounds

Condition

Condition births life
Condition freezes water
Condition melts water
Condition boils water
Condition bends crayfish
Condition bakes potatoes
Condition boils potatoes
Condition fries potatoes
Condition makes us happy
Condition makes us sad
Condition brings about death

Jah Rastafari

The God that must feared
The creator of the heavens
Moulded and sculpted the earth

The king of king, lord of lord
The conquering lion of Judah

Our father and loving creator
We give praises and worship
Singing, drumming, dancing…

Life and Death by Palmwine Sounds

Badman Lighter

I am a madman
I am a court case
The Badman go light am
Enter Kirikiri prison
Bleed dancing,
As the wipes sing
Like a true madman
Speaking wise word
Shouting on social media
Most using me to catch cruise

Baba

A true Casanova extraordinary
A true lover of the African Queens
Him plantain no dey stay one place
Cruise dances to ashawo melodies.

Youths

The Youths of today
Are the leader tomorrow

Today youths, are stubborn
Today youths, have wised up

Youths are elders of tomorrow
Youths are ancestors of tomorrow

Elders shall not manipulate
Ancestors can be wrong

Create paths for ourselves
Elders may choose to guide.

Creators

The universe is our canvas
Mould and craft to our well
Drawing inspiration from-
Past, present, and future.

Pain

Pain builds character
Smile with pain
Laugh with pain
Sing with pain
Dance with pain
Love the pain
Embrace the pain
At the end, smiles.

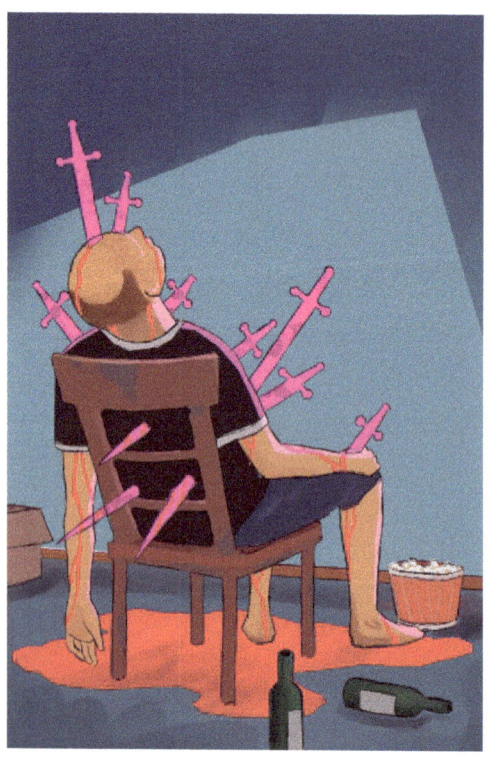

Chaos Show

Yanga on bassline
Trouble on percussion
Shakara on horns
Wahala on the keys
Angry Lion on the mic

The tail has been touched
Consequences unpredictable

Lights, camera, action
Hope you enjoy the show.

Being a Man

Women can never truly understand
Battling the world and its virtues daily
Our innocence and pure heart chips away
To provide for our Queens and Princesses
And protect our Queens and Princesses

Always fight silent battles
Even hidden from mum
Encouraging ourselves
Lock the pain away, And
Pick ourselves from the dirt.

Mistakes

Mistake is not always mistake
Mistake is a new invention
Mistake is a new idea
Mistake is a new science
Mistake is a new breakthrough
Mistake is a new discovery
Mistake is a new journey
Mistake is a new formula
Mistake is a new music melody
Mistake is a new dance step
Mistake is a new recipe
Mistake is a new solution
Mistake is a new life lesson
Mistake is a new way of doing something
Mistake is character development

Ginger

Loss of motivation
About to give up
Pat on your back
Pick yourself up
Ginger the swagger
Because cruise awaits.

Fisher men

Patrol the sea of women
Using your tongues as bait
If one no catch, cast again
Changing the bait periodically
Because no two fishes are the same

Hustlers

Entrepreneurial spirit guides
Founding members of the,
Money Men Association

Sacrificing for the future
Investing funds for growth
Still very under appreciated.

Wicked Game

Want to play the wicked game, Remember
Your deck deals only physical damage
Mine deals both physical and spiritual
I May appear to be losing at the start
My spiritual cards are just powering up
Spiritual damages deal physical too.

Rest

The smooth jazzy melody called rest
Periodically the money song must be paused
Smooth jazz called rest, might bore some
Tempted to keep playing the money song,
Remember, human body is not firewood
Or, in pigin, body no be firewood, brother.

Life and Death by Palmwine Sounds

Marijuana

The international herb
Persecuted for been free
Smoked from Africa to Asia
It grows in Europe and Australia
Helps the Americans economies

Let the herb be free
Smoke it in a rizla
Smoke it in a chalice
Sativa to Indica
To each their own
It holds no malice.

Life and Death by Palmwine Sounds

Different shades

Different shades, one specie
All different shades of brown
Some a lighter or darker shade

Same blood flows through veins
Am spare parts for my neighbours
My heart can beat in your chest.

What is within matters the most
Packaging design by Jah Jah
The soul is what defines us.

God dey Create

Some beauty pass beauty
God shows off sometimes
Bring out his golden pencil
And sketches a work of art
Creating the definition of beauty.

Jah Guides

Let him steer the wheel
Just enjoy the journey
Its smooth and bumpy
Jah on wheel, cruise.

Jah Jah Blesses

With Jah on the wheel
Just pray and smile
All problems dissipate
Blesses in abundance.

Praise Jah

Received blesses
Give him praises
Worship humbly
Cup runneth over

Not Ordinary

I REPEAT
GOD FORGIVE ME FOR MY PRIDE

One leg in the physical
One leg in the spiritual
Am a mysterious man

MOST SHALL NOT UNDERSTAND
I AM WHO I AM

Father

Jah is the father of fathers
Disturbing, with your problems
Father would guide and support
Solving problems, you don't know
Fighting private battles for us
Always remember to give thanks.

Otedola

Otedola with the money
Major share holder, of the
Money Men Association
A smile that befits a chef
Money no sweet, nah lie
His Queen and princess,
All bliss, Cuppy chop am!!!
What is all hard work for?

Beauty

True beauty lies within
The flesh is eye candy
The heart defines beauty
Beauty lies in character.

American Military

Let's put aside all the negatives behind
Let's put aside the political chess games
The American Military gets shit done
Red, white, and blue, built on morals
I would never want to be an enemy
Even if I win, my loss would be massive.

Stubbornness

Free the madness
Madness is free
Tap it like Palmwine

We want what we want
We would find our way
Don't test the stubborn

We are called revolutionist
We are called black sheep
We are called prophets….

Life and Death by Palmwine Sounds

Knackademos

Him prick nah compass
Knackdemos no get type
His true north nah yansh
Rizzinator is his second name
Any shade, size, height…
Knackdemos shall conquer
Ashawo melodies on repeat

True Madness

True madness is quiet
It does not yell or scream

True madness acts sane
Because its raw madness

Present opportunities
A glorious show awaits.

Drum and bass

Reggae drives weary
It fights downpression

Veins become the bass strings
The heart chants the nyanbingi.

Ska to the reggae
Funk to the reggae
Swing to the reggae
Move to the reggae
Rock to the reggae
Wine to the reggae.

Trust

Trust humans?
Wickedness
You shall get

The heart of man is evil
Kind people distance,
Is my advice to you.

Don't let them ruin your heart
They would manipulate,
And disappoint you.

Ikebe

The healing factor of the nations
No matter my wearies and problem
As my eye lay on them, it dissipates

Small yansh, looks so appetising
Big yansh, bump to the rhythm
Cruise sings and dances to Ikebe

Holy Mount Zion

On the road to Zion
Must tread Babylon
But with thee as armour
Babylonians repelled

At Zion gate
Praises,
Worship,
And gratitude.

Ghana Men

The Ghanaian brother
Always super ecstatic

Wake up at dawn
Site one soft Ikebe

They can't be blamed
Ikebe fights downpression

Cruise Nation

'Democrazy' made us crazy

A nation fuelled off cruise
Light, water, road, no dey

Tribal discrimination
Religious discrimination

Cruise sincerest prayers

Life and Death by Palmwine Sounds

Wahala

Attention! Attention!
Wahala is set free

Entered market
Buying trouble

Everything must scatter
Chaos has been set lose

Cruise watching, eating maize.

Funk

The funkinators on the stage
The baseline moves the waist
Tapping our feet to the drums
Sprinkled with some percussion
The keyboardist calls on horns
Lead guitarist catching his cruise

Jah Soldiers

Put on your helmet
Which are your locks

Lightning as weapon
Frightening wicked

Our eternal mission
To destroy Babylon

Fight for truths and rights
Destroy the hopes of wicked

Looking on to Garvey
Who has gone before

On till the Zion gates calls
Rasta men shall tread on.

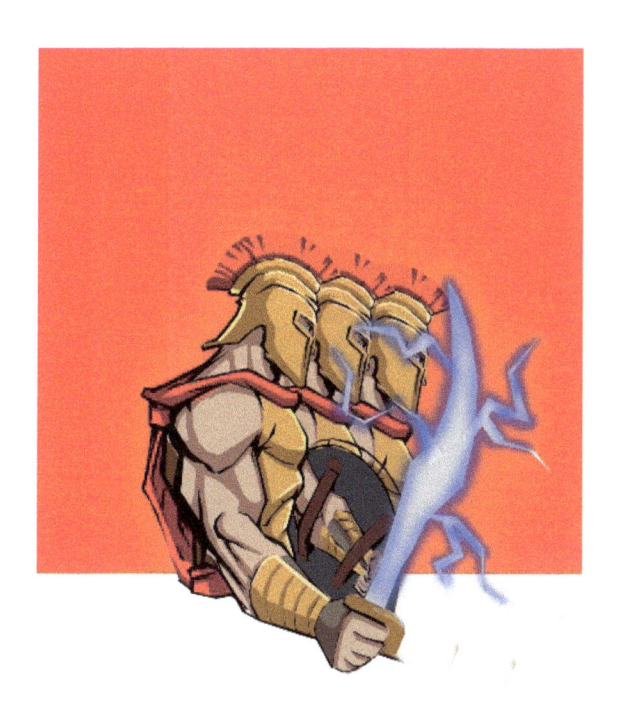

Heavy Rotation

Grind it, roll it, lit it
Roll one, roll two, roll three…

Steady on rotation
Eyes blood red.

Chasing vampires.

Life and Death by Palmwine Sounds

No Condition is Permanent

Brother man don't be weary
Jah is steering the wheel

Why downpress yourself
Just smiles and prayers

Current times might be tough
Smile at what the future holds

Smile

Today might hurt
Emotional rumble
Frustrated, irritated
Downpressed, saddened
Overthinking, Worrying
Crying silent tears
Just smile for the future
We all fight hiding battles.

Life and Death by Palmwine Sounds

Yansh is my Religion

Cruise our head reverend on pulpit
Santamonossca (Speaking in tongues)
When I was a youth, I followed breast
Rabatalasaraka (Speaking in tongues)
But as a man the back side is brighter
Orofutocosotoka (Speaking in tongues)
Men of Culture can I hear a loud IKEBE!!!
Yayoratocasato (Speaking in tongues)
Choir play the ashawo melodies on repeat.

Ashawo

Ashawo no be work
Nah management
No be talk am ohh
Nah Saint Augustine

Ashawo no get type
They get schedule
Fishes meet, choas
A very cautious person.

The Most High

Jah is the highest of the high
Communicate with the highest
Likewise, man must be high

Some are high on life
Some connect with herbs
Some go into meditation

Sunday Rice

Sunday rice hits different
Every other day it's norm

Maybe it's the anticipation
Maybe it's the pastor's blessings

All I know is when I get home
I shall consume double portions.

Living The Highlife

Cruise showing the path
High on Mother Nature
Sufferation eliminated
Downpression eliminated
Wickedness eliminated
Babylon has crumbled
Treading the road of life
While death accompanies.

Hushpuppi

Minster of Cruise
And Cruise
Related activities

There papa, mama
Sister, brothers
All go feel am

I no come to suffer
Legal or illegal hustle
Jah is my final judge.

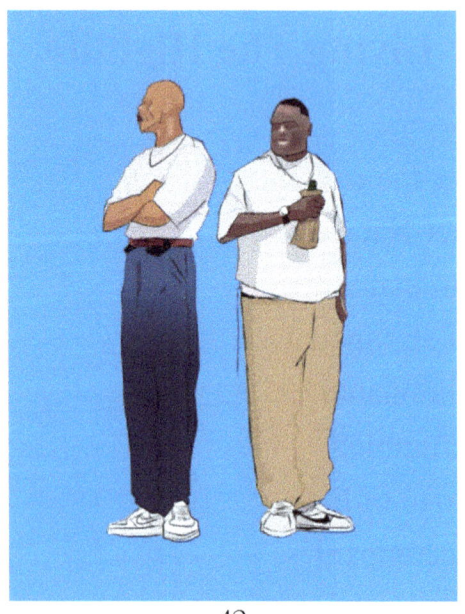

Milton Keynes UK
Ingram Content Group UK Ltd.
UKHW052114251024
450245UK00009B/553